THE

EMPATH

AND

PSYCHIC GUIDE

A COMPLETE BOOK FOR DISCOVERING & DEVELOPING YOUR ABILITIES, GIFTS, EMOTIONS AND PROTECTING YOURSELF FROM NARCISSISTS AND ENERGY DRAINERS

Disclaimer

The information contained cannot be considered a substitute for treatment as prescribed by a therapist or other professional. By reading this book, you are assuming all risks associated with using the advice, data, and suggestions given below, with a full understanding that you, solely, are responsible for anything that may occur as a result of putting this information into action in any way – regardless of your interpretation of the advice.

TABLE OF CONTENTS

CHAPTER ONE: INTRODUCTION

Studies once showed that Highly Sensitive Persons make up about 15%- 20% of the World's population. These set of people either live their lives in fulfilment or misery. The latter are people who have had to develop specific strategies to get the best out of life and the latter being people who never had the opportunity to undergo a process of managing the challenges that come with their nature or finding essence to life. Another perspective on the latter is that, a number of these set of people who make one-fifth of the world's population do not even know they belong to this category.

Since you are reading this book, congratulations! You are not giving a chance to misery. Whether you have realised that you are an empath or not, this book is a complete guide to figuring that out and to start you on the journey to greatness for good! It is a complete and practical guide on how to become a balanced, empowered, and happy empath. To live your life to the fullest as an empath, you must learn ways to prevent picking up the emotions of others. You also need to know how to communicate with your loved ones, co-workers and even peers on how best to relate with you. These and more are what I will show you in this book.

There are millions of books written to help empaths discover themselves and get more out of life. Do you know what makes this one different? It is the simple, orderly and detailed approach to presenting the reality of empathy in such an irresistible manner. This is not simply a productivity hack, or a motivational book about self-discovery and maximizing one's ability. It is targeted to help empaths find a sense of living. There are facts provided in this book from reliable sources and with real examples that can help you through all the ideas presented therein. That being said, this book is a more practical approach to maximizing your skills and abilities as an empath. This doesn't include in depth philosophy or psychology but offers you techniques and insights as an effective and empowered empath.

For each chapter, you get to learn something tangible with well-attested facts. The first chapter introduces you to the whole idea of who an empath is and their identifiable traits. The second chapter proceeds to share insights into embracing and developing one's empath gift. This part also gives non-empaths the guide to developing empathic abilities. This book entails a complete guide as it also takes you through how to get the most of your relationships in the third chapter. The fourth chapter gives you a guide for getting healing through natural remedies.

Each chapter presents new thoughts, ideas, facts, examples and tips all targeted towards giving you a more level-headed knowledge about you and how you can get better! The ideas are offered in a sequential order that builds on the previous ones. They are like unlocking a safe; you will have to get all the numbers in the combination in the right order. It is advised that you go through every word, sentence, paragraph and chapter as they are perfectly connected to leading you to that perfect destination.

Depending on your choice, you may want to read this book through all at once for you to get a complete idea of all the process covered in the book before you begin acting on them. You may also decide to read a chapter at a time, then take your time to practice at your pace. If you figure that you're already familiar with some of the guides here. That's great! You know what they say about repetitive exposure making new ideas a part of you. I hope you enjoy the adventure!

CHAPTER TWO: ROAD TO DISCOVERY

While growing up with my parents in my youthful skin, I was very sensitive, determined and highly spirited. I remembered the way I cried during movies and at commercials. I made friends with every child in the neighborhood and worried about them all the time. I usually thought that there was something wrong with me, for being "weird"- too kind and empathetic. I always had a listening ear for anyone willing to share his/her problems with me. Years later, my empathetic personality has brought great impact to my life, relationships and professional development. I have been able to fully understand the beauty and curse of being empathetic. I have been able to channel this ability for my benefit. My compassion has been of my strengths.

This chapter encompasses all you need to know about being an empath. There is a full and detailed description of who empaths are with a highlight of the various character traits displayed by them. One beautiful thing about the reality of empaths is that they differ among one another. You will also gain insight into the traits that distinguish empaths from each other and how they can be identified.

 Being an empath makes you feel the world deeply and that affords you a view of the world in its immense beauty and love. However, it does not exclude you from the feel of the ugly and cruel sight of the world. The only thing is that you can control the view from which you decide to see the world. Here's to telling you that even if you are not an empath, you can begin working on developing empathic skills to your own advantage. This chapter also explores how you can do that without leaving you blank on how to embrace the gift of empathy fully.

WHO IS AN EMPATH?

An empath is one who has a strong intuition and picks up the moods, intentions, desires, energies, wishes feelings, motivations and thoughts of others around him. It is an inborn trait with the ability to tune in to the feelings of others. Being an empath is associated with high sensitivity and emotions; they intuitively know the intentions and motivations of others and making it seem as though they are continuously bearing the burdens of people around them. There is this usual saying of Empaths wearing other people's headaches.

Empaths have a unique personality with a high sensory level. Most times, people tend to refer to them as mystical and magical creatures. Some say, being an Empath is similar to a holding a powerful spiritual title. They are characterised by the awareness and sensitivity to the energy levels of people and even animals around them. Some extreme empaths also tend to have the capability to heal others.

Empathy is the gift and ability to put yourselves in the shoes of others and feel things the way they do. It is also important to clarify that being sensitive and being empathic does not always mean the same. An empath happens to belong to a category of sensitive people.

Not all highly sensitive people (HSPs) are empaths. Empaths have large hearts and they become loyal friends and mates. They are passionate, creative, and in touch with their emotions and can see the big picture. They resonate with nature and often love water.

Aletheia described the empath to have such a great level of sensitivity which gives them that unique ability to figure out the emotions, needs, feelings, pain and even the thought patterns of the people around them.

After reading my description, I bet one person that readily comes to mind is the character of "Deanna Troi" on *Star Trek: The Next Generation.* She portrayed strength, brilliance, a degree of sensitivity, and a great deal of psychic knowledge and telepathic tendencies. We can go on to mention the likes of George Orwell, Mahatma Gandhi and Mother Theresa who displayed clairsentience in their lifetime. Maybe being an empath is not a bad thing after all! An empath who doesn't understand their gift may find it overwhelming to live productively due to the burden of carrying so many emotions. Let's take a look at some of the traits displayed by empaths.

THE MAJOR TRAITS THAT YOU PORTRAY AS AN EMPATH

- **You feel the emotions of others and you tend to bear them**: Tracing the origin of the word; empathy which comes from the Greek word "em" meaning "within," and "pathos" meaning "feeling." This implies that, empathy is the ability to feel the feelings of another within ourselves. This is a huge one for empaths and it's one of their primary traits. The empath's ability to pick on other people's emotions ranges from some being able to pick the emotions of people around them and some can even sense what is happening to their close ones from afar. Other people's moods affect you and sometimes you find it hard to distinguish what is your own mood and the one you picked from others. You have mood swings frequently because you occasionally mirror other people's mood and energies. Extreme empath and those who pay more attention to their sensitivities will know if someone is having bad thoughts about them, even from great distance.

- **Picking up physical symptoms too**: Beyond the known fact that empaths pick up the feelings of others around them, they tend to develop the physical ailments of people around them. They tend to feel other people's pain and pick off illness such as common cold, eye infections, and pains in different body parts. Empaths experience this especially those they're closest to, while taking care or nursing them. In addition to this, there are certain health conditions usually prevalent among empaths, such as chronic pain, depression, or auto-immune deficiencies.

- **The tendency to know**: Imagine having impressions about people even strangers and they turn out to be correct. Empaths tend to know things without being told. You have the ability to figure out the feelings and thoughts of others. It also transcends to your ability to know when you are being lied to. You would not easily fall for a dishonest or a deceptive person. Your guts would easily substitute for a lie- detector. You also feel wronged when people lie to you.

- **Public Places are overwhelming**: Have you discovered how much you always avoid public places? It is very normal for you to avoid crowded places and gatherings such as markets, mobs, malls, parties, nightclubs, or the stadium where you find a lot of people around. You tend to avoid such places because you tend to feel the emotions, moods and turbulence from people you find in such places. To make it worse, you cannot help such feeling.

- **Love and Need for solitude**: Quiet times are very essential to empathic people and they regularly crave for solitude. You know how you long for a retreat to a personal space in your home without any light or sound and other things you are sensitive to by nature.

- **The sight of violence or tragedy is usually unbearable**: If you find out that you distance yourselves from watching violence on the TV or reading about it in the newspaper or even the sight of cruelty on the street. You definitely portray one trait most empaths show.

- **You are Compassionate**: Another trait you should look out for is how you are drawn to people who are suffering, emotionally distressed, marginalised or downtrodden. You easily show compassion to others and people in turn would want to offload their problems on you. You don't usually talk about yourselves to others but you genuinely love to learn, know and care about others. As a result of your listening ability, you become a dumping ground for everyone else's issues and problems which later ends up as their own.

- **Extreme and Constant Fatigue**: Empaths often get easily fatigued. They feel the weight of the world on their shoulders which is caused by being drained of energy, either from energy vampires or taking on too much from others. Despite your fatigue, you can't help it saying no to people who need your help.

- **Easily drawn to nature, babies, pets and animals**: It's normal for people to see babies and pets as being adorable. However, empaths sense this attraction on a different level. You feel a special bond with nature, babies and animals. You cannot withstand seeing an abandoned animal without rescuing it or a tv commercial showing impoverished children. You tend to talk to nature and animals, because they understand you. You typically keep pets in your home.

- **Interest in Spiritual Art and Metaphysical Activities**: Empaths have a natural inclination towards the metaphysical such as meditation and Yoga. They get fascinated by topics relating to dreams, angels, spirits and fantasies. They are also involved in activities such as hypnotherapy, organic nutrition and psychic reading. People feel that empaths have a special connection to the unseen realm and heaven and they are often regarded as mystical creatures. They are suitable to act as spiritual advisors because of their healing abilities, profound spiritual hypersensitivity and intuitive nature.

- **You have an Addictive personality**: Another trait portrayed by empaths is their tendencies to get addicted to things such as alcohol, drugs, sex, tv shows, music or even a person. With these addictions, they tend to block out the emotions of others and to numb the pains empathy presents them with. Their addictive personality also serves as a form of self-protection in order to hide from someone or something.

- **Adventurous by nature**: Empaths love adventures. This explains why you are always looking for the answers to unanswered questions and your constant drive in the pursuit for knowledge. I earlier described emphatic people to be free-spirited people who love freedom and travels.

- **Boredom Sets in easily**: You get distracted and bored easily especially for things that don't engage you. You find it difficult to hold your focus on things that don't stimulate you. You get easily detached and often resort to daydreaming in that detached state of mind. For you, life, home and schoolwork has to stimulate you or your physical body gets separated from your mind. You find it convenient to stare into space for hours, in a world of your own.

- **Hates Routines**: Being free spirited, empaths find things that deny them freedom as debilitating. They hate rules, routine or control and they always want to have the freedom to do what they want to do when they want to do it. Whenever they are being controlled or expected to follow routines, they feel imprisoned and restricted.

- **You can feel everything including the days of the week:** There is the funny weird feeling empaths pick up from virtually everything. Sometimes you have the ability to relate a particular feeling to every day of the week. You know when it does not feel like the usual Monday. You can tell how the world is feeling collectively on certain days as well. You more than any other person can feel the heaviness that comes from certain days of the week such as Mondays and Tuesday, mornings.

- **Even your food**: One major character portrayed by empaths is that they are so easily drawn to things and tend to attach or pick a feeling from everything including the ability to sense the energy of food. I have heard different stories of empaths who don't like to eat a particular food products especially animal products because they can feel the vibrations of the animal.

- **You can't hide your feelings**: Empaths do not know how to hide their feelings. You present yourself to people the way you feel. You hate to pretend about your feelings. Others can tell exactly when you are happy or sad. You detest trying to be happy when you are not. I mentioned earlier that empaths tend to have mood swings which often portray them as introverts, unsociable or even miserable.

- **Attachment to New Things**: You must have discovered how much you preferred new items to used ones while shopping. Empaths will prefer buying new items to buying antiques or second-hand because to them such second-hand object carries the energy of the previous owner. Although this trait is not exclusive to empaths alone but it's one trait to look out for due to ability to pick emotions even from objects.

In order not to bore you with an exhaustive list. There are still some other unique traits to look out for in empaths which you will discover among other things being discussed in this book as you read further. All empaths do not necessarily have to exhibit all of these traits mentioned at the same time. There are some common traits such as hypersensitivity to the feelings of others, intuition among other major traits. Take a quick test with these questions; Answer either Yes or No to each of the questions and take note of your response.

THE QUESTIONS?

1.) Do you feel you are highly sensitive?

2.) Do you feel easily overwhelmed by crowd, public places, bright lights or noises?

3.) Are you deeply compassionate and feel

compassionate to help the weak, oppressed and vulnerable?

4.) Do you regularly have mood swings and feel as though the weight of the world is on your shoulders?

5.) Do you feel drained among certain persons and they feel energized?

6.) Do you have trouble distinguishing other people or things' emotions from your own?

7.) Do you know how someone is feeling without being told?

8.) Have you found yourself constantly taking alcohol or drugs or participating in some activities (exercise or TV) to avoid pain?

9.) Do you think you live more "in your head" than in your body?

10.) Does the suffering of babies, animals, or other things from nature hurt you deeply?

11.) When someone near you has a physical illness or body pain, do you feel it in your body?

12.) Do you dislike reading the newspaper or watching the news, scary or sad movies altogether?

13.) Do people usually see you as a peacemaker, counsellor or their advice-dispenser?

14.) Do you often crave solitude to retreat or lighten your mood?

15.) Do you find interests in topics on the unseen realms, spirits, angels, fantasies and metaphysical?

If your response is yes to most of these questions and

probably a bit unsure about others, then you are an empath and you are on your way to full discovery! However, if you think many of these questions do not resonate with you, do not fret. You may not be an empath but you are capable of developing yourself to become one. There is a part of this book specifically designed for how to develop the empathic gift.

MILD, MODERATE OR EXTREME EMPATHY

You need to determine your level of empathy. Identifying the degree to which you are an empath will clarify your needs and the specific energy management techniques you must know. This is important to make you effective, productive and happy. Also, your level of empathy depends on the number of traits you can identify with. It is important you discover what degree of empathy you fit into order to recognize how to manage yourself effectively.

There are MILD, MODERATE and EXTREME empaths. If you have given more negative responses to the questions above, you are likely to be a Mild empath. Being a MILD Empath shows that you have a partial empathic tendency and barely have those traits mentioned above and you seem capable in control of your feelings.

If you have as much positive responses than the negative responses, you are a Moderate Empath. Being a MODERATE Empath reflects a normal level of empathy and you sometimes find it difficult to manage the energies in the world, but with the right guide, you can manage through life incredibly.

However, if your answers to those questions have been all positive. Then you are an Extreme Empath. As an EXTREME Empath, you discover that you are extremely sensitive. With a strong empathic tendency, you can utterly be totally overwhelmed. A full- blown empath finds it difficult to navigate through life while being able to feel so many energies around you. Don't get discouraged, it just makes it important for you to learn and develop good energy management practices so you can thrive and enjoy your life.

Having discovered your level of empathy, we will go further to learn the various types of Empath for you to consider which ones resonates with you the most. By gaining detailed understanding of your empath type, it helps you identify and control the energies that affects you more than the others which don't.

CHAPTER THREE: WHAT TYPE OF EMPATH ARE YOU?

We have different types of empaths. These empath types are distinguished by the various set of empathetic abilities in existence. This understanding will help you streamline your discovery to your specific gifts and abilities. You will also be able to assess your strengths and your lows for optimum living. There is also the possibility that you are able to relate with one or more of these types. As you read through the details provided for each empath types, you should be able to evaluate your empathic abilities based on the scale I will provide. The possibilities are; You **do not feel** that an empath type applies to you, that **you slightly feel** that an empath type applies to you, that you **definitely feel** an empath type applies to you. Keep in mind that you may fit into many of these types, or fit into only one empath type. Empaths exist with varied and subtly distinct sensitivities.

Let's go ahead to consider the ten (10) major empaths types that exist and figure out which is peculiar to you:

1. EMOTIONAL EMPATH

This is the most prevalent category of empaths. They are prone to pick up other people's emotions and mirror such feelings, either positive or negative. An emotional empath has the ability to feel the emotions of other people. Many times, this makes it difficult for them to discern their own emotions from others. It could be devastating for emotional empaths to experience emotional neglect because their emotions affect them deeply. They may have been labelled as too emotional. They are heart-driven people and tend to be shoulders of comfort to a lot of people including strangers because their intuition helps them respond rightly to other people's emotions.

2. PHYSICAL EMPATH

Have you discovered that you pick other people's physical pains such as headache, sores, pains, cold, stomach ache, flu, itches, or any other discomfort they feel and tend to absorb them into your own body? Then you are a Physical Empath. In the same vein, such empaths can also pick up the physical wellness of others. Physical empaths can feel another person's physical pain or illness within their own body and on a positive side, they can also get energized from the sense of well-being of others. Whenever physical empaths come in contact with sick people either as caretakers, they'll feel it. This may not be immediate; the empath will feel one or many of the symptoms within their own body. which they can then use to promote healing.

3. LOCATION EMPATH

Location empathy is a situation where a person has certain physical or emotional episodes which is caused as a direct result of the person's presence at a certain location. It is possible for location empaths to feel anxious, depressed, exhausted, or even have physically pain while visiting a location where a tragedy or negative situation occurred in the past. Similarly, location empaths tend to also get joyous or happy visiting locations that has occasioned such in the past. Simply put, location empaths are drawn to energies or vibrations from places they visited.

4. PSYCHOMETRIC EMPATH

This category explains the nature of empaths who have the ability to receive energy from impressions, statues, photographs or other objects. Psychometry relates with been able to receive psychic information from object by holding or touching it. Due to a high level of sensitivity of an empaths' sense of touch, they feel things through their sense of touch and most times they feel they can communicate with these objects.

Further, the psychometric empath tends to pick up information not only by touching objects, but also through touching people around them and other living things.

5. COLLECTIVE CONSCIOUSNESS EMPATH

These are the world's burden bearers. This type of empaths are people who are sensitive to not just the emotions of not just one person but a group of people they have come in contact with. This category of empaths is usually drawn to a collective set of people in their neighborhood, workplace, city, state, country. Some of them even pick up emotions of the whole continent or planet. Those who are sensitive to the collective consciousness will feel the fear, separation, shame, despair, and suffering of the entire collective group. This type of empaths usually find themselves attuned to issues affecting the world such as Climate change, pandemic, politics, violence, oppression, or war.

6. ENVIRONMENTAL EMPATHS

These empaths are known as Geomancers. An environmental empath is drawn to changes in weather, atmosphere or other natural occurrences which causes a shift in his or her emotions or cause them to experience physical symptoms. These ones have the ability to feel earth's vibrations or energies. By intuition, even when they don't realize they also tend to react when a natural disaster is about to happen. These reactions could cause them to have mood swings.

7. TELEPATHIC EMPATHS

Telepathic empaths show strong intuitive tendencies. They possess the capability to communicate directly through extra- sensory abilities which includes precognition, clairvoyance or other psychic means. They are able to get information about others by intuition. Most people tag it as the ability to read the minds of others. They also exhibit the ability to know what is to be done in any given situation and most times this is often coupled with a feeling of calmness during crisis. There's also the aspect where some telepathic empaths also have Precognitive tendencies. This means that they get premonitions of future events in their dreams or even when they are awake. Telepathic empaths receive intuitive knowledge from their dreams or from sensing an occurrence which they utilize to guide themselves and others.

8. SPIRITUAL / MEDIUM EMPATHS:

This category of empath can feel and sense ghosts and spiritual beings. This ability needs to be sufficiently managed or otherwise it can disrupt the person's life by causing depression, exhaustion, frustration or even serious physical illness. Spiritual empaths can feel the energy and the presence of spirits. They use their mediumship abilities to see into the past, present and future of others' life. They are attuned to the spiritual energy surrounding people, places and things. Spiritual empaths usually have a sense of connection with spirits, the dead and even angels. They are inclined to spiritual activities such as hypnotism, meditation, fortune telling etc.

9. ANIMAL EMPATHS:

These are empaths who can feel the emotions or even physical pain of animals. Animal empaths tend to sense the emotions of animals and talk to them. They feel they understand the animals and they have a strong connection with them. They find it unbearable to see a suffering or impoverished animal and cannot withstand seeing similar pictures or videos. Such people also pick up interest in studying biology or psychology of animals. This empathic ability could also help an empath build his gift in healing animals, animal care or wildlife conservation. One perk of being an animal empath is also the fact that having a pet really can help absorb negative energy or feelings you may have picked elsewhere.

10.   PLANT EMPATH

A plant empath is someone who feels drawn and have a special relationship with plants. Like Animal empaths, they can feel and intuitively get information from plants. They can sense the needs of plants, they believe plants have emotions and share a deep connection with them. They sight of a suffering plant tend to hurt them.

These are the major categories existing, however there are other rare categories such as the cosmic empaths who are affected by the energies of planets, cosmic ray and geomagnetic storms. Having identified the kind of empath you are or your empathic abilities in case they are more than one. Many empaths exist because they were born that way. However, there are many others whose empathic gifts were borne out of traumatic experiences during their childhood or while getting older as adults. There are some empaths who developed this gift as an outcome of some of their habits and practices such as energizing exercises or spiritual practices which reinforces this sensitivity pattern in them. Essentially, for you this gift may not be innate but you can develop it.

In case, you discover that you don't exhibit any of the traits highlighted or any of the categories mentioned. You may need to develop the empathic gifts. We will be looking briefly at how you can develop the empathic gifts.

CHAPTER FOUR:GUIDE TO DEVELOPING

The Empathic gift becomes a must have for human beings to survive amongst each other. It is a necessary tool to aid the relationship with fellow humans.

Empathy, by practice is a skill that can be cultivated and improved. Those who don't have the innate abilities of an empath can learn empathy as an art. Empathy is the act of understanding and feeling the emotions of another person, and thereby responding accordingly. Empathy differs from sympathy or pity. It is about gaining cognition of other people's experience as if it were being experienced by oneself. Empathy is necessary to gain social skills, to understand other people to share and show responsibility and to help others without judging. The ability to connect to and to understand one another's point of view helps us build the kind of connections that sustain us and lead to happiness, better health and productivity in our day to day relationships.

Empathy remains an indispensable virtue for our individual, physical and emotional survival here on earth and it is important that one cultivates the skill where it is not inherent. I agree with Meryl Streep who identified the empathic ability as a great gift possessed by everyone because we all at one point or the other share an emotional link to certain persons around us. Even when you're not feeling it, there are certain processes that can be employed to improve or develop your empathy level. Study has shown that empaths or empathic people are more likely to function well in the society and they have the right people's skills to solve problems, whether at school, their workplace or addressing issues facing humans generally.

In order to develop empathic skills or abilities there are certain processes non-empaths must pass through. These processes also double as stages of the process an individual goes through while building empathy. These stages in the order to which they are meant to occur are; acting, meaning, imagination, perspective-taking, feeling and understanding. An individual who wants to develop empathic skills is meant to and can experience all of these stages. The empathetic process is said to be a circular process because they may not surface in the order given above. In other words, these processes vary in individuals and some stages may even surface before or after they are meant to emerge.

Certain factors may also influence the process and the occurrence of each of the stages in each individual. Such factors include; the nature of the empathetic situation experienced, the nature of the person who intends to develop empathy, and the extent of preliminary information that such a person has before the stages. We will then go ahead to consider how these processes/ stages work.

First, the acting stage embraces the notion of placing oneself in other shoes. This process occurs when the person who empathizes tries to stimulate his or her feelings while trying to understand others. While this individual takes up acting, he needs to attach meaning to the feelings of the other person he is trying to understand. This is what the meaning stage entails.

Further, the imagination process is a special communication aspect of developing empathy. It is the union of images, senses and thoughts. This process relates to creating images of oneself on a probable or improbable situation. In this aspect it is creating imaginations based on the feeling you are giving meaning to.

Further to this is the perspective taking process which relates to the ability to take cognisance of the special situation or condition of other persons or groups. This process goes beyond creating meaning or imagining, it is understanding the reason the reason a person thinks or feels the way they do in given circumstances. This process is important to developing empathy because it is necessary to understand their perspective to develop empathy for them. Progressively, the stage of feeling comes to fore.

Feeling relates to taking cognisance of the affective part of understanding others and their perspective. Here is to sensing how the person you are concerned about is affected by the conditions they are in and the perspective they take of those conditions. Then, you are able to recognize behaviours that appear to be extremely emotional or unreasonable as simply a reaction based on a person's prior experiences.

There is also the process of understanding which is the last stage of developing empathy. It has to do with comprehending and being thoughtful of situations of other people. This is also the central process of the empathy development stages.

Summarily, the process runs whereby a person gives meaning to his experience first by acting empathic in a way that he tries to place himself in that same position. The person may then create images and sights of being in the other person's shoe. He also goes further to evaluate from that person's perspective and then share their feelings. As a result of this processes, the person can then understand by anticipating the feelings and thought of that person and even go further to imitate the person and can sympathize with him or her.

This process was made simpler in Daniel Goleman's

classification of the elements of empathy. He identified five elements which entails Understanding people, helping them develop, serving others, attaining diversity as a leverage, and political awareness. I will attempt explaining these elements briefly.

By understanding others, you tune into their emotional cues even the subtle ones. This is made possible by listening well and paying attention to their non-verbal communication. This reflects that one is able to help other people based on their understanding of their needs and feelings. The concept of understanding as also been explained earlier.

Another element is Developing others. This means you are able to act based on people's needs and concerns and subsequently helping them to reach their full potential. You tend to offer people constructive feedback by rewarding and praising people for their strengths and accomplishments making them figure out how to improve. This also entails mentoring and coaching others for their development.

Similar to the above is the fourth element which is having a service orientation. a service orientation means to look for ways to improve people's satisfaction to whatever you do and their loyalty. This element explains the approach to 'go the extra mile' for people to meet their needs.

In addition, leveraging diversity means interacting with everyone based on their peculiar needs and feelings and being able to create opportunities through different kinds of people, recognising and celebrating differences in people. People who do this respect and relate well to everyone, regardless of their background and they see diversity as an opportunity to make people with diverse nature work together for common good.

Finally, Political awareness has to do with being able to pick up and respond to the emotions of a group of people and the way they relate with themselves based on power. These elements to finding interest and understanding the feelings of a group of people who share common perspectives and thoughts. Political awareness can help individuals to navigate organisational relationships allowing them to achieve where others may previously have failed.

To develop empathy productively in your workplace, give your co-workers, bosses or subordinates your full attention, always look out for verbal and nonverbal clues to help you fully understand them/their situation. Set aside your own assumptions; see things from their own perspective, acknowledge their feelings, allow a deep introspective and emotional connection, then take positive action that will improve their situation and create an effective synergy.

The above explanations have shown that through developing certain good people and relationship skills you can develop empathy or work being towards more empathetic.

CHAPTER FIVE:EMBRACING YOUR GIFT FULLY

Having talked about the different empath traits and types that exist and also given full guide into developing the empathic ability in the case you figured out you are not an empath, you need to realise that you don't have to hide your sensitivity but you need to embrace your full abilities and gifts as an empath. There are a lot of people who have discovered themselves "to be too sensitive" or "too emotional" as most empaths regard themselves and have not yet developed the mind-set to accept their true nature and embrace their gift. This part is to help you understand that you need to embrace your gift fully.

Most empaths were born extra sensitive; they could see, feel or hear beyond what others sense. Some people also grew up to be like that because of their traumatic childhood or adulthood experience. However, embracing what would have been a curse and recognising it as a gift. They have been able to use their gift to take control of their energy, tune into the feelings of others and even those that abused them as a tool of survival. However, many empaths never learn to embrace the gift and tune the focus back to themselves and find a way to empower themselves and use their gift to be the healers they have been destined to be.

The most rewarding part of one's journey in life as an

empath is learning to understand one's gift and not seeing oneself as a victim. A lot of people have maximised this gift to create wonderful opportunities for themselves and also to help others understand this wonderful gift like I am doing now. There are a lot of persons who have made good life coaches, counsellors, leaders, spouses, spiritualists who do the readings and energetic healing all in a bid to empower people empaths and non-empaths to shine their own light.

If this part of the book resonates with you, all you have to do is to decide that it is time you take responsibility to embrace this gift fully and work on yourself to achieve the desired results. Taking responsibility for yourself is a great step towards self-love, empowerment and using your gifts as an empath. You do not have to depend on anyone else to make you feel good about your nature. Even if people will accept you and understand you, the giant step has to be first taken by you. Also, no one outside of you can make you do or to behave in a particular way if you do not feel good about yourself. As empaths, it's very inherent to think we need to be the caretakers of the feelings of other people and not care about our own. That is the major misleading thought that denies you the chance to get better or shine your light and make you good to no one.

The goal is to embrace your gift by connecting with yourself more by paying attention to your feelings. It is vital to make time for yourself in stillness, so you can find clarity and the answers to your own questions. You will also need to meditate in order to release strong resistance to going with your own flow and keeping up with who you are. This really is about being in your real and better self for the world so everyone can benefit and the responsibility is entirely yours to take that step and continue to take consistent and productive steps that keeps you in alignment. This is the major key to personal development as an empath. Eventually, you will find yourself in favorable circumstances and around people who will allow you shine your light instead of you hiding your abilities.

You should also learn to take regular breaks for relaxation and deep breathing exercises for stress relief. Avoid being in environment that is overly stimulating as much as you can and when you cannot avoid such overstimulating places ensure you take your time to be mentally and emotionally prepared beforehand. Such overly stimulating environments may not even be physical places. For instance, the Social media and internet are overly stimulating environments and you should often take a break from the energy that is emitted through the internet. It is also advised that you have a regular routine in place for activities that you enjoy doing that relaxes you and brings you relief they could include; reading books, getting a massage, taking a warm bath, using or inhaling selected fragrance to boost your mood-aromatherapy.

Embracing your gift will also require you to build authentic, deeply connected and intimate relationships. To do this, you will need to have clear, loving and honest conversations with people. Express how you feel more and you will evaluate those who truly wants to be associated with you and those who do not. As you take to staying present with yourself and your true nature and staying aligned while shining your own light, one of the scariest thing that will happen is that you will notice a pivotal change in your relationships. The relationships found on love, acceptance and truth will thrive and remain while those built on fear, lies, dependency and hiding your true nature will cease to exist. In the process of developing yourself, you will have to learn to let things go – such as the latter types of relationships I mentioned and give yourself a chance to be happy. Some relationships – the viable ones, will definitely get better when you show up as yourself. You will find it easier to thrive and it will be much more fulfilling in such a relationship.

Another reason to embrace rather than shy away from your unique abilities is to help you discern your feelings from other people's feelings. This can be made possible when you set boundaries for yourself. A major challenge empaths face is the inability to set boundaries. This is what makes it impossible for you to identify with your own feelings. How does this work?

As an empath you tend to pick the energy and emotions of other people or things and you find it difficult to put your own feelings above others. You will need to get clarity about what works for you and what does not, and then it will get easier and easier to distinguish what feelings are yours and that of others. You can now notice the energy and emotions of others but not take them on as your own, you stop being the victim of other people's energy and you can now assist others with your intuitive ability in your own unique way.

I know thoughts are already running through your mind. You are already thinking of how you want to embrace your gifts but you are afraid you are too sensitive. Or you don't know how to heal or you don't even know where to begin. This is why this book is to guide you through understanding your gift as an empath and discovering your sense of self.

CHAPTER SIX:UNDERSTANDING YOUR GIFT

This is where a natural curiosity about your ability sets in, you want to know what your strengths are or what your strengths can be if you develop yourself. You also want to know your weaknesses and things you will need to protect yourself. This what understanding your gift implies. Once you start to embrace your gift and understand the positive and negative sides to your nature, you are able to know what direction to channel your efforts in and also the situations you should avoid or protect yourself from. Understanding your gift also makes you discover what roles perfectly suits your empathic nature and what involvements would bring you to the positive side of life. You should know at this stage that every empath would adequately qualify for roles and positions that requires listening, inter-personal or social, high emotional intelligence, mentoring, conflict resolution, leadership, passion and excellent communication skills.

If you are thinking or doubting whether you actually show tendencies to have the above-mentioned skills or not, it is because you have not yet fully understood your gift and unique abilities. Through your past encounters and experiences, you are fully aware of how deeply energy and emotions can take its toll on you either negatively or positively. This makes it essential for you to understand the energies that you carry and how you can manage the energy around you.

Learning how the energy you possess as an empath works is a thrilling adventure, and it can help you see through a myriad of possibilities in life. As you have read earlier in previous parts of this book, many empaths become light bearers. These are the people who have learned how to embrace their gift and gone further to understand how their energy can be maximised to help them live their life to the fullest. There is much more to being an empath than you have read about so far. Your journey to productivity has just started. As you read further, you will continue to understand and know how to enhance your gift, meet the right people, avoid the wrong people and learn more on how to manage your gift and unique abilities.

This part of the book is one of the most important part of your journey to finding your sense of self. It is to help you understand that you are not insane, that you are good in your own skin and that you can live a happy, healthy and fulfilling life.

First, we are going to consider the positive side and the downside of being an empath.

CHAPTER SEVEN: THE DOWNSIDE AND UPSIDE TO BEING AN EMPATH

We are kind, loving, nurturing and we make up the best people you'll meet. Sometimes we get overwhelmed coping as an extroverted empath and dealing with too many people or too much all day, so we need time alone to rejuvenate ourselves. We pick the energy of people, colours, things, music and virtually everything. That in itself can be exhausting. –Barbara Benton.

I am going to start this part of the book discussing the negative sides to being an empath. I have written at length so far trying to encourage you to embrace your gift, quit shying away from your unique abilities and to develop yourself as an empath. I have also gone ahead to encourage you to develop empathy in case you are not one. Now we need to talk about the weaknesses, lows and downsides to being an empath. This will make the book balanced as to exposing you to the not-so good aspect of being an empath. However dear empath, this is not to discourage you but to make you see the things that may be dragging your productivity or hinder you from shining as light and we will go further as you read the book to explore ways you can manage these aspects.

DOWNSIDE 1: PICKING OTHER PEOPLE'S EMOTIONS

The ability to feel other people's emotions may be a pretty unique ability. But like most of other things in life, there are both positives and negatives to feeling other people's emotions. It is not the actual fact that you are directly experiencing the emotions of those around you that makes it a negative thing, it is the inability to pick and choose what you feel that makes it potentially dangerous and can be energy sapping, both emotionally and psychologically, making you end up battling with pain and confusion. Whenever you are around people who suffer anxiety, depression, fear, sadness, or stress, you tend to experience same with the sufferers first-hand– without being able to control it. This right here can make the empaths experience devastating sometimes.

DOWNSIDE 2: HIGH TENDENCY TO FEEL OVERWHELMED

In addition to lacking control over the feelings empaths pick up, they can also become easily overwhelmed by tragic news, heavy noises, bright lights, strong smells, coarse fabrics, blasting sirens, busy or crowded environments. Looks like a lot of things to avoid? Intimate relationships can also be overwhelming when empaths tend to mirror the energy in that relationship especially when their partners do not live up to their expectations. They can also be overwhelmed by their partner's needs. Also, empath parents often feel overwhelmed and exhausted from the demands of child-rearing because they tend to absorb their children's feelings and pain especially at their formative years. For empaths, this tendency can make being a spouse or a parent totally exhausting.

DOWNSIDE 3: YOU BECOME OVERLOAD

After discussing the two major downsides to being an empath, we should also discuss your tendency to become an overload of emotions and information. First, your listening abilities makes you prone to bearing the whole world on your shoulders as everyone tends to "offload" their problems and worries on you and you tend to bottle them all up. While being a problem-solver and counsellor to others, you are also likely to build up a shield for yourself by not letting in others on your thoughts and feelings thereby causing you to bear more emotions than you ought to.

In the same vein, empaths are always on the unending look for knowledge and answers to their many unanswered questions. They tend to know a lot about many things and many people which can in turn lead to information overload. The disadvantage of being overload with information is that you may end up being overwhelmed as discussed earlier. You may also find it difficult to make decisions and in most complex cases you may experience a brain fog.

As an empath, your ability to feel love and compassion for others is on a different level.

DOWNSIDE 4: YOU ARE PRONE TO LOSE YOUR SENSE OF SELF

People who do not understand empaths have unnecessarily tagged them as being "overly sensitive" or "too emotional" or "extremely compassionate" and in many cases have prescribed how they ought to live and behave because they are seen as "not being in charge". Intuitively, empaths also have the tendency to reflect the behaviour of other people around them without the intention to do same and this is disadvantageous because they tend to lose their true selves in the process.

Worried about these demerits? You don't have to! Be rest assured that all these downsides can be effectively managed or avoided however the case may be. Interestingly, the upsides to being an empath outweigh the downsides and they reflect the innumerable prospects of developing and embracing your gift.

THE UPSIDE OF BEING AN EMPATH

What is it that they say about looking at the bright side of things?

UPSIDE 1: PICKING UP THE FEELINGS OF OTHERS.

Yes! You read right. Seeing that the major trait of empaths is their ability to pick up the emotion of others, it sure has a lot to tell on why there is both a positive and a negative side to it. The tendency to mirror the emotions of others is a great side to empathy. This trait can help improve both intimate and distant relationships because empaths can see from their perspective and understand them better. The empath is uniquely designed to have the ability to detect and deeply experience the feelings of others. This trait can be highly beneficial in your workplace, you could sense if your co-workers are feeling inadequate, you can pick up on that intuitively than a normal person and offer support. The same would work for an anxious date, you could sense how they feel and help get them along with you very well. You possess the unique ability to relate to others deeply and in a way that is unconventional.

UPSIDE 2: THE TENDENCY TO BE LOVING AND COMPASSIONATE

You possess traits that helps to better identify with other people- their feelings and emotions including those you'd normally disagree with. Many people may find it difficult to understand the feelings of others even when they explain how they feel, but an empath cannot relate to this. An empath can easily resonate to knowing what it is like to walk in other people's shoes.

The gift of compassion is an innate ability in empaths. When you learn to "take charge" of your nature, you will realise you have a lot of good to offer both for yourself and your loved ones.

Empaths find themselves give meaning to being in other people's shoes and this allows you to find a common place with people and peaceful way. This trait can also make you a good leader. No wonder we were able to identify earlier, a number of great leaders in their own times were figured to be empaths.

UPSIDE 2: TENDENCY TO ACTUALLY FEEL GOOD ABOUT YOURSELF.

The exhausting and overwhelming situations empaths face may actually place them on their lowest and they may feel lower than even normal. Bad side? The best news is that they have a tendency to be in their highest and feel highs that are even higher. Being an empath, being in your lowest could signal an allowance for your soaring highs. You see, you have the innate power to feel really good which can even last for a lifetime.

UPSIDE 3: THE EMPATH AND HIS CREATIVE ABILITIES.

Empaths happen to make a majority of the most creative, innovative, intelligent and witty people we've got in the world. If you are an empath, you may want to consider gaining relevance or earning an income following creative pursuits. Empaths are usually an embodiment of useful and creative ideas. Their creativity is often expressed through dance, acting, painting, music, creative writing, drawing, spiritual excercises and bodily movements. Empaths have the sixth sense to deeply appreciate good music, work of art, paintings and sculptures and other creative works.

You can also easily give meaning to the emotions of the makers of those creative works. As an artist, you are drawn by the raw beauty and emotion denoted through a paint brush and clay. Similarly, a music piece speaks to you on a visceral level. Empaths will also suit as perfect storytellers due to their imaginative and creative nature.

UPSIDE 4: YOU COULD FIT IN FOR A LIE DETECTOR.

Being an empath gives you the capacity to detect lies. Even the seemingly little white lies. You can easily figure out when your partner says they are okay when they are not. Interestingly, you cannot be easily deceived or cajoled. Whether or not you will consider this as something beneficial to have, I believe detectives or investigators who are empaths will find their job much easier.

UPSIDE 5: YOUR HAVE DEEP PASSION FOR THINGS AND THAT'S ALRIGHT!

Empaths usually exhibit passion and deep-seated love for people, babies, animals or nature with a driven commitment to help or improve them. The good side to being passionate about these things is that you can channel this passion to live a rewarding and fulfilling life. This explains why most empaths are often tireless teachers, volunteer, caretakers for our environment, pets and wildlife. Many empaths have the ability to sacrifice their personal time to help others even at the expense of payment and accolades. Empaths are passionate and dedicated to things they are drawn to and can easily channel that passion as a drive to enjoy life and their choice of work. Passions are usually the drive for empaths who show tendency to stay committed to what they love doing and may even get totally lost in such an involvement.

Other positive sides to being an empath include that empaths make good leaders for their charismatic nature, they make good diplomats, and they are natural healers. I hope seeing the nature of empaths "Upside Down" must have propelled you to want to get better and develop your unique abilities. If it hasn't, you may want to still consider doing other things that will be mentioned subsequently in this book and discover yourself along the line.

CHAPTER EIGHT: NORMALIZING DAY TO DAY WITH YOUR GIFT

This part of the book is to make you see being an empath as the new normal and for you to know how to cope with being highly sensitive in your daily living. This will involve you learning the consistent habits, practices and process to make the gift a part of your life on a day to day basis. When you go through this normalizing process, you are making a bold decision to fully embrace your gift as an empath and to discover your sense of self. At this stage, you will have the mindset that it is normal to be emphatic and you will be able to use it for your daily benefits. You will discover hacks to managing your sensitivity and emotions and build habits to tune in and out of emotions anytime you want to.

First, you will have to quit getting bothered about whether or not you can tap into your unique abilities but admit the fact that you are an empath and you have the capability of living normally and getting the best of your uniqueness. You will also need to stop seeing yourself as one who cannot take charge or who is being held back by his abilities, this part is to empower you to know how to manage yourself and adjust to normal daily living even as an empath. You don't need to come off as a mystical or "weird" creature to people around you.

In addition to self- management, this is also a step to making people around you understand who you are and posing yourself as being in charge and making others know that it's okay to be the way you are. It is also living to make people live by your own rules for the sake of protecting your energy and emotional health. It's also good to make people realise that being uniquely fashioned is not a bad thing, after all humans in the world were not made from a cookie-cutter factory.

Empaths will need to know their personal biases, what brings them to their lowest, how they can find strength and become stronger. This stage is a continuous process that requires determination, and perseverance. This wouldn't require you to stop things that you will normally do or that every other person who are not empaths do because you find them overwhelming, exhausting, energy-sapping or confusing. It is not the case that you will stop reflecting all the emotions of people around you as you used to but going through the normalising process will help you live with those things you can identify with, and this time you will be able to avoid those things affecting you negatively. You will only pick the emotions that you want to and you will be able to discern your personal feelings from that of another person.

This is about you, your partner, spouse, workmates and other people around you getting used to you living your life as an empath. You are able to regularly recharge yourself and feel energised and empowered without the usual experience of you feeling drained, overwhelmed or exhausting or moody. You can still direct your nature in a manner that you decide for it to, to get the best out of life and to help others with your unique and psychic abilities. You are a natural healer and you can do this while being able to discern accurately people's emotions and without having to mirror those emotions yourself.

One unique thing about the normalisation stage is that you will have to practice all the hacks and exercises you will learn here consistently. Consistency is the only key to helping you get accustomed to these processes because getting used to them is the key to normalising and mastering the empathic gift. Some things are necessary for you to do while normalising this gift and they will be discussed in detail under the following sub-headings.

ALLOW TIME FOR SELF-REFLECTION

For the empath to act serenely, sanely and objectively, he needs to get to the point where he understands himself and knows what makes him tick. He needs to be able to identify his feelings and bring his consciousness to distinguishing how he feels at different situations. This is the first step in the process of taking control of his actions. This is to say that self-reflection will result in self-awareness and subsequently leads the empath to ultimately take control of his actions.

If we are going to attach a meaning to self-reflection, we will define it as the act of sitting back to think or ponder seriously. To the empath who intends to normalize his gift it is a process that requires frequent, deep and honest self-examination. The act of self-reflection reflects the understanding that self-awareness, self-care and self-love are at the core of our well-being generally and even as empaths. This is to also help you accept yourself and gain confidence in being in your own skin. Daily self-reflection routine would improve people's well- being generally if practiced and for empaths it's not a mere recommendation but it is a necessity for wellbeing. As empaths' understanding of themselves deepens consistently, they are able to synchronize with their real nature and they become more fluent and free flowing with their unique abilities. While you are able to connect with who you are and you are able to identify with yourself. That feeling of alignment can produce ultimate joy for you.

Self-reflection also reflects the power of developing oneself and empowerment that lies within for empaths and this is the reason it is essential to check within on a consistent day- to- day basis. Self-reflection should be practiced daily and this should be done at least once daily but practicing twice daily is highly recommended. The suitable moment for such self- examination should be very early in the morning before you do anything at all and before you go to bed in the night.

The times recommended are strategic because self-reflection in the morning will help you figure out residual emotions and experiences you cannot let go of and to realize the feelings attached to your mind that you are unconsciously holding on to. It's been studied that most of such emotions comes to play in our dreams. Such reflections in the morning will then allow you to let go of such feelings capable of holding you back from positive energy and robbing you of the best you can get from your daily experiences.

Then in the night, you are able to assess your emotions and evaluate your reactions based on the situations or things that affected you the most during the day. The night is a good time to reflect before going to bed because the experiences had throughout the day will still be fresh. You will be able to detect how these experiences have affected you and release them so that you can have a peaceful and restful sleep. It gives you the chance to also analyse your feelings and make resolve on how to make the best of the next day's experience and also take gradual healing approach towards the unusual and rare events of the days.

For non-empaths who intend to develop empathy as well, it is good to implementing a morning and evening self-reflection routine to examine yourself as this will strengthen your compassion and understanding for others.

Let us go ahead to talk about the various effective methods for self-reflection. One effective way to self-reflection is Meditation. This will be the first method we will consider, co-incidentally because it also serves as the foundation for processing one's feelings and to regulate the brain. There are a lot of things you will need to know about meditation and don't forget that practicing consistently is key.

MEDITATION:

Meditation is an effective method of self-reflection which is a sacred practice of spiritual discipline used to relax the mind, align with the divine realms, and to build Life-Force. In a twelve-part series for empaths, meditation was said to be an art that can help you balance and align your chakras (energy centres), to connect to the higher and spiritual realms, protect yourself and to rid your aura of any negative energy. Meditation will help you deal with negative energy, help you centre your energy and focus.

There are various forms of meditation sourced from different climes, traditions, religions and traditions which are innumerable and cannot be exhausted here. There has also not been a standard or a resolve for the best or most effective technique of meditation. You can as well practice more than one technique over time for your physical and mental well-being. However, a few techniques will be discussed here which can be suitable for empaths and It is advised to explore various techniques to meditation and find a practice that you can get accustomed to. Mira Dessy agrees that one practices a meditation style "that feels comfortable and what you feel encouraged to practice".

These seven types of meditations were compiled by Ashley Welch and was medically reviewed by Dr Justin Laube. It should be noted as said earlier that these types mentioned are only a few among the numerous types of meditations in existence and you can do well to learn about and explore other types.

1. **Mindfulness Meditation**

Mindfulness as the name implies which means being aware of where one is and what one is doing, and not being overly reactive to what's going on around one, entails a meditation process of being fully present with your thoughts. Mindful meditation can be practiced in various locations. However, some people prefer to sit in a quiet place, close their eyes, and focus on their breathing. Mindfulness meditation requires you to reflect on your thoughts, feelings and emotions however, you let those emotions and thoughts pass without judgement.

2. **Transcendental Meditation**

Transcendental meditation which is also known as mantra meditation prescribes a simple technique of meditation in which an individual picks a mantra which can be a word, sound, or a small phrase to be repeated in a specific pattern during meditation. For instance, the common mantra used by people is the "om" sound. This is to allow you settle to a profound restful and relaxed state. This kind of meditation is prescribed for a duration of 20 minutes twice daily and can be carried out while sitting comfortably with the eyes closed.

3. **Guided Meditation**

Guided meditation as opposed to unguided meditation is one which entails a meditation technique led by a teacher or a guide. Guided meditation is also called guided imagery or visualization because it requires you to employ your sensory organs in creating imaginations that you find relaxing. It is a meditation technique which requires you to use your sense of sound, smell and touch to form images or scenarios in your mind for a calming effect.

4. Vipassana Meditation

Vipassana meditation is an ancient Indian meditation technique from which the mindfulness meditation technique is sourced from and studied to have dated back to 2500 years ago. The word "Vipassana" suggests the meaning; "to see things as they really are". The goal of this meditation technique is to achieve a personal transformation through self-examination or self-observation. It is aimed at creating a deep body and mind connection which is arrived at by a focused disciplined attention to physical sensations in ones' body. On the long run, you tend to create a mind balanced with deep expression of passionate love and compassion. During the time of practicing this meditation technique, you are required to stay away from certain habits such as stealing, lying, killing, sexual activities or using intoxicants.

5. Loving Kindness Meditation

The Loving Kindness Meditation otherwise known as Metta meditation is the practice of reciting certain words and phrases to illicit warm-hearted feelings and direct good wishes to other people. This meditation technique requires you to sit in a relaxed and comfortable position, taking few deep breaths and repeating certain words. First, you have to focus on yourself and repeat some good wishes to your hearing. Such as "May I be well. May I be happy May I be at ease. May I know peace." Upon doing this for a while, you will then start to imagine people close to you or who are related to you and direct the mantra to them. Now you replace the words "I" with "you." Finally, you end the meditation with the words directed to the whole universe such as: "May all being everywhere be happy." This meditation for helps you develop love and kindness to others.

6. Chakra Meditation

Chakras, of an Indian origin is translated to mean

"wheels". It is believed that the life force that moves inside everyone is spinning like wheels. They refer to the centers of energy and power of spirits in ones' body. Studies show that to be seven chakras. Each chakra is

located at different parts of the human body which are the heart, the throat, the third eye, the sacral, the root and the sacral chakra which are accompanied with a corresponding colour.

Chakra meditation entails relaxation techniques aimed to bring health and well-being to the chakras in the body by bringing one's imaginative attention to the various body parts.

7. Yoga Meditation

The yoga meditation is a technique of practicing

various calming exercises in comfortable positions. This technique which dates back to ancient India entails a wide variety of controlled breathing exercises intended to promote flexibility and calmness. The positions for this meditation require balance, full concentration and less distractions.

Empaths creating personal rituals such as meditations ensures a sense of stability, as well as helping you meet your physical and spiritual needs in solitude. You should also avoid falling asleep in meditation as this does not make meditation practices effective. Meditation is a powerful tool to help us focus on the body and empty our minds of any negative emotions. You don't have to feel as if you are in control; there is no stress and you can enjoy your energy at that moment.

DEEP BREATHING

Noticed deep breathing is indispensable even in meditation? Deep breathing is a necessary activity for empaths. You gradually and deeply, inhale and exhale air through your lungs on a regular pattern. This is because as you withhold your breath avoid breathing deeply, you have the tendency to keep uncomfortable energy within you.

Deep breathing is cultivating a patterned breathing exercise to be carried out on a structured regular basis which allows you to relax your mind and body. There is no recommended frequency for carrying out this exercise but a normal deep breathing duration suggests breathing in for 5 seconds, after which one withholds one breath for 6 seconds and then breathe out for 8 seconds. Also, the exercise can be carried out at any time of the day. While doing this you can imagine any negative energy leaving your body with the air. Deep breathing is a known method for focus achieving the harmony required within.

As an empath, this is one self-reflection process that uplifts you and recharges you as you feel energised after taking deep breaths. During this act, you do not feel the pains and distress of others. In this state, you appear off as untouchable by emotions and the energies around you and the good thing is you can always come back to this state of being. The breathing pattern you build based on your intuition as an empath also helps to put distress away. Don't forget empaths are natural healers.

The shorter or longer our breaths are, is always dependent on our reactions to the situation we are in. This explains what happens when a person is afraid or is in a stressful position and begins to have shorter breaths. By having a regular deep breathing exercise daily helps to relieve the body of its' stress, detoxify the blood, reduce tension, pump oxygen into the blood, helps to achieve a sound sleep pattern and causes relief and balance to the body. As it is with every new habit, your body tends to correct its breathe patterns.

A good deep breathing pattern helps empaths attain the ability to get a total charge of their emotions and redirect it to their energy centre. One hack to get yourself out of distress and get relief in any overwhelming situation is to practice deep breathing regularly!

GROUNDING

Normalizing your abilities as an empath also requires that you ground yourself on a regular basis. Grounding is a key to achieving balance as an empath and allows you to regularly get rid of negative energy and redirecting you to your energy source. This act requires coming in deep contact with the earth as a means of finding one's root. It entails touching the earth with one's feet or whole body to undergo the earth's healing process. It is studied that grounding is crucial for one's wellbeing and while being in contact with the earth's electrons it helps to calm our nervous system.

Self-reflection is aimed towards you gaining and becoming self-aware of your nature and the force of the earth that backs one up. Interestingly, such self-reflection happens when you root or ground yourself in a particular space and this is one benefit of grounding. It's suggested that one can practice grounding physically in various ways, it ranges from allowing one's bare feet connect with nature by walking on a bare land or walking or laying one's body in a grassy yard. Other ways of grounding include; exercises such as low back and abdomen exercises, cuddling, platonic or non-platonic hugs, wearing your cosiest sweater, restorative yoga which is a meditation practice that relies on gravity; which is the original grounding force, to stretch and strengthen your body, taking a bath, all of these things will root you into your nature and in turn strengthen self-appreciation and self-love.

There are also other emotional or spiritual ways by which you can practice grounding. These practices include; Discussing your feelings with someone who will not judge you- a professional therapist, forgiving yourself or writing in a journal. Being grounded strengthens the energy centres that are often weakened by an empaths' uncontrolled emotions.

SET BOUNDARIES

While discussing the empaths major traits and

downside, you discovered that empaths finds it nearly impossible and difficult to set boundaries. It becomes necessary while normalising one's gift into the day-to-day living to know how to set personal boundaries. It is important to set boundaries for an empath to maintain a balanced and productive life. First, an empath needs to understand the meaning of boundaries. They are the limits one sets to restrict himself from doing or accepting certain actions or situations. You should think of boundaries as rules you set up personally to protect you in sensible ways. Of course, they are bound to change as the empath grow and face changing circumstances. It is also not expected that the same boundaries apply to different empaths.

Setting boundaries will need you to learn to create time

and give yourself space. This ultimately leads us back to an empath's need for self-reflection. Self-reflection will also help an empath define boundaries for himself. Also, setting boundaries will require you to properly communicate your needs to others without a sense of guilt. It will also require that you figure out what serves your highest good as distinguished from what serves the good of others to your detriment. This is not to make you selfish but to guide decisions you will need to make based on your feelings and emotions. Creating boundaries for yourself will also require you to separate situations that affect you personally and situations that does not affect you directly but affect other people which you pick up their emotions.

By setting boundaries, you are able to distinguish your

personal pains, thoughts, emotions and energies based on your intuition from those you pick from being drawn to other people or things. The goal is not to prevent you from having the ability to pick up the emotions or thoughts of others which you will naturally do. Rather, you know when to focus on yourself or when to react to the needs of others. You will know what help you can render and when to say no to things that are to your detriment. It has been studied that empaths tend to give in to helping others even at their own detriment. They constantly accede to devoting their time and energy into helping others and end up feeling overwhelmed, drained and exhausted.

Setting your boundaries will not empty you of your compassion or passion for things or people but rather strengthen you to share your compassion when it is alright for you to do so without feeling drained or exhausted. This will be more fulfilling and comfortable. It is also beneficial to help the empaths maintain emotional and mental balance and to develop true love by first loving oneself. It is an unchanging principle of life that you may find it difficult to love others if you don't love yourself.

I would have hope learning about this normalisation process would just be enough to attain the peak in living excellently as an empath but you cannot just get comfortable attaining normalization stage but you will need to be consistent and remain positive while going through all these processes to avoid staying stagnant or face retrogression in the journey to discovery and sense of self as an empath. To live in deep and constant

harmony with your unique abilities; create time for self
-reflection by ensuring you meditate daily, take long walks in gardens, talk to a friend who is non-judgemental, keep a journal; it aids in sorting out which emotions are yours, and where the rest are coming from.

CHAPTER NINE: PROTECT YOURSELF

"...Knowledge and understanding is the key to defending yourself against such beings. When you understand what you are up against, and how they operate, then it's much easier to deal with them." – Gary R Leigh.

The empaths sensitive nature makes it important for him to build protective shields against certain practices, people and things and that is what this chapter is about. After understanding your unique abilities as an empath, you should progress to mastering the tides and waves of your emotional energy, you will need to be careful about being tossed about by external factors without finding a firm stand for yourself and your well-being. You are without doubt a gift to the world, who needs to feel appreciated, welcome and valued by those around you – a world that desperately needs what your unique intuitive abilities has to offer.

Up until now in this book, I have been giving you complete insights and details on knowing your true natures and tendencies. I have also gone further in making you understand how to make the most of living by aligning yourself with your true nature and most certainly enlightened you on the fact that you will need to protect yourself from certain things you are prone to such as information overload, exhaustions, addictions, fatigue or feeling overwhelmed. Now you need to etch protective fields around you. It is about an empath developing resilience while exploring his or her unique gifts of emotional sensitivity and compassion without being overwhelmed or exhausted. It is not just about protecting yourself from other people's energies but avoiding other factors that may drain or rid you of your own energy.

Other than resorting to addictions as most empaths are prone to, in order to avoid or block of certain emotions or feelings, it is much better to actually stay away from the real source of the pain or negative feeling. This is showing the crucial part of protecting oneself from certain things. You will need to learn effective strategies to help you avoid distress and negative energy from others and to protect yourself from narcissists and other energy vampires. You will need to position yourself to build in protection to gain a sense of safety as It is important that the empath feel protected and safe.

Generally, empaths will need to learn the art of shielding themselves as soon as they find themselves in situations not pleasing to themselves. This chapter may not be able to fully cover all the possible situations or things you need to protect yourself from but it will guide you into knowing how to build protective walls for yourself in similar situations. Protecting yourself is not also about controlling people or things that you vividly do not have control over. It is not the case that you will need to bother yourself about changing the things you cannot influence but protecting yourself from such things. The work is on yourself to "grow a thick skin" around things you cannot change that may want to spread negative energy around you.

Setting up a protective shield around our body, like using white & coloured light energy shields can block energy being absorbed from others and act as a protective shield. Although this may not work for everybody so you may need to explore whether or not it will work for you. Others also believe in spiritual activities like praying to build a protective shield. One way that this can be done is to invoke the Archangels to create a shield around you. You can say a prayer by invoking Archangel Michael who is believed to have strong protective qualities to keep you safe and protect you at all times. Lamanda Brown gives an example of a prayer format to invoke archangels for protection like

this;

"Dear Angel Michael, I ask you to please protect me, my

family, my home and those who I love with your

powerful shield. Surround me in your purple light,

which allows only pure love to penetrate. Please stay

with me day and night and keep me (and my loved

ones) safe. Thank you."

Asides from using the white light and making prayers

of invocation, there are some natural remedies which

one can use to protect himself or herself from negative

energies. This will be discussed later in the book.

However, we need to learn about protecting oneself

from energy vampires and narcissists. You will need to

read this crucial part of this book to identify these

energy drainers and also learn how to protect yourself

from them.

CHAPTER TEN: PROTECTING YOURSELF FROM ENERGY VAMPIRES

If by any means you are related to any energy vampire, you need to know how to protect yourself. They are referred to as energy vampires because they feed on and suck off other people's energies. An energy vampire is defined as anyone who drains other people's energy; they are also called energy suckers or psychic vampires. Some people become energy vampires intentionally while some others are not conscious of what they do.

Christiane Northrup, M.D. gave a study report that

about 20% of all people (male and female) have full blown vampire characteristics. This signifies that one in five people in the world are energy vampires. She also went further to analyse that one of each of these energy vampires affects other five people in the world which implies that close to 60 million people are directly or indirectly affected by energy vampires. This also reflects the likelihood that everyone is related to or has come in contact with an energy vampire.

Energy vampires are those you are in a relationship with that are capable of exhausting or draining you of your energy. Studies also show that empaths or highly sensitive persons are more prone to relating with energy vampires as family members, workmate, partner or close friend which you may not even be able to limit your contact right away. The worse part being that some of these energy vampires are people who actively seek out people like us and tend to take advantage of how much we care. We may not even figure out quickly that we are even in a relationship with one. This is why self-protection should be your primary goal when dealing with energy vampires and this makes this part of the book important for you to read.

These are some strategies you can take to protect yourself from energy vampires:

First, you need to realize that energy vampires exist and most of them even double as empaths. We empaths do not believe the existence of bad people and this explains why we always persevere even in toxic relationships and keep covering up for others. Empaths are highly intuitive persons, so you should trust what your intuition says about people around you and pay close and detailed attention to that instinct. If your intuition avoids someone, you can keep a record of how those people behave. Ensure you also pay attention to how they treat people they meet because that also says a lot about them.

You should also be able to double check your gut-instincts with a friend. Find a friend who knows you well, who is clearheaded and trustworthy and who has not been taken in yet by that person who is an energy vampire. Do well to reach out to that friend to figure out your uncertainty about such energy vampires.

Further, self-love as we have talked about is important to embracing and understanding your gift. You need to learn to put yourself first. Energy vampires tend to always want to be in control in their relationships with you. They are overly- assertive and manipulative in nature and can often be aggressive. Always put it at the back of your mind that your needs and feelings count too and you should base your relationships with energy vampires on this. Energy vampires can also downplay on your abilities or your successes and empaths on the other hand, give too much praise or credit to others. The lack of reciprocity of this nature in your relationship with energy vampires can be extremely exhausting. So, you should practice how to always give yourself the credit for the good things you do even if it is not publicly. Learn to pat yourself regularly on the back. Another aspect of self-love necessary for empaths to protect themselves from energy vampires is to appreciate yourself regularly for who you are and for the things you do or are doing well.

As we have also discussed earlier, you should say "no" when it is not alright for you to render an assistance. You should know when to turn people down especially when a particular assistance you are needed for is at the detriment of your health and well-being. Although empaths find it difficult to turn people down but it takes practice. It is high time you stopped saying "yes" all the time. If you cannot say no, you can give it time and while deciding your response remember your feelings count too!

Energy vampires in neighbourhoods or workplaces are good at putting one person against another. This is why you need to distant yourself from petty neighbourhood or workplace gossip and do not get close or socialise with toxic people. This is why we discussed setting boundaries in the last chapter. Setting boundaries are important to define things that you are going to involve yourself in while relating with others and things that you would not. Know that you cannot relate with everyone similarly. Like I first mentioned, energy vampires do actually exist. There is always that friend wants to complain about how things are not going well with others or their friends, or who wants to vent about a recent breakup or loss. Understand that you cannot bear such negative emotions for the whole of the time. Put a limit to the time you spend with such persons. Get back fully into your emotions after you are done with them and gradually learn to let go of those negative emotions.

We know you are passionate about your work and the people you are devoted to but understand that there could be energy vampires among them too. This is time for you to place priorities on your mental and emotional health before work calls. Empaths need to remain aware of the effect of their work obligations on their energy levels and emotional wellbeing. Whether you work as a therapist, or any job that requires you to relate to a client who might be going through a difficult time and can leave you exhausted, depleted, and even depressed. Learn to ground yourself at intervals while relating with such people. Learnt to also practice other activities that you enjoy outside work to relax and rest. Alongside learning to do what you enjoy outside of work is creating a quality alone time. During this alone time, do things that help you shed off all the negative emotions you must have picked from people while being with them. Always take a few minutes daily to engage in activities that helps you achieve a balanced and healthy lifestyle. You can decide to meditate, have a warm bath, or walk through a garden.

Prioritise your relationships and pay attention to the people you spend more time with. If you know someone who drains your energy while you spend time with them, stay away from them. Energy vampires do not consider others and neither can they offer the reciprocity necessary as a solid base for healthy relationships. You should not allow a relationship to drain you than it re-energizes you. An empath's relationship with others thrives in love and compassion not self-sacrifice or lack of reciprocity.

CHAPTER ELEVEN: PROTECTING YOURSELF FROM NARCISSISTS

The other set of people empaths must protect themselves from are narcissists. Empaths by nature, put others before themselves and unless a trained and empowered empath, most empaths do not know how to love themselves. Imagine such empaths being in a close relationship with someone with an entirely different nature from themselves. Think of what a relationship between someone who places himself extremely above others will look like with someone who extremely put others before himself. Wouldn't that be counter-productive? Well, it should be but an empath can learn how to protect themselves from such people especially when they are an indispensable part of our circle.

Narcissists are everywhere around you. This is why this part of the book is important. Science shows that narcissists actually make good business owners and they help business growth however most of these professionals let their self-love run wild especially to the detriment of their colleagues or people who work under them. An empath needs to understand and learn the nature of this kind of people before he knows what he is dealing with and how to protect himself.

A narcissist is an egocentric person and a self-absorbed person. He shows extreme admiration and love for himself above any other person and has the tendency to be proud and selfish. Such a person is wired to control, manipulate and be an emotional predator. They could be of any gender or age. Narcissists will always work hard to be right and would not believe they can make mistakes. They may even go to the extent of denying their mistakes, even if you put out their mistakes before them. They do not listen to advice, and they are often doing their own thing. Most of them who are close friends with empaths can be energy drainers because the empaths tend to give up their time to advise a narcissist but still goes ahead to do whatever he feels like and ends up running to the empath again to tell them their woes.

Empaths can also easily fall prey to the manipulation of

narcissists because of their nature. This is why it is important to know how to deal with them. Let us go ahead to know how to protect oneself from narcissists.

First, avoid arguing with such people. There is no point arguing or exchanging words with them because that will only drain. As much as you can, just nod and go your separate ways. Avoid spending quality time with them for the sake of your mental and emotional well-being.

Where narcissists make your boss in the workplace, they would want to demand for your attention, where this cannot be avoided, do not let the time spent with them control or drain you. You can practice grounding especially placing your barefoot on the ground when you are with them. This is to help you focus on your energy centres.

Also, admit that you need support and get it. Narcissists may also drain you of energy and like you do to energy vampires; you can check in with a trustworthy friend. You can also reach out to professionals to help you. For instance, you can consult a psychotherapist who specializes in helping those who have experienced narcissistic abuse. Their assistance can be beneficial in this kind of situations. There are different vampire split groups that you can join to help you in protecting yourself in this regard.

Sometimes, you may decide to help a narcissist go through the transformation path. This will require you to employ your listening skills because narcissists would not want to hear you out unless they have been heard. If you are going to help them get better, you will need to get narcissists get to a point where they can listen to you. This would not happen until they first feel you have listened to them. Big work, isn't it? Narcissists need healing and that can only take place when their mind is in a receptive state.

You should also try to avoid expending your energy on someone who is not ready to heal. If they are not in a receptive state and you keep making efforts, you may end up being exhausted and drained. They may even make you look as a failure and you need to avoid anything that puts you in such a state. You can't heal someone if they are not in a space to accept it. Some narcissist can be dealt with you just need to know how to protect your energy from such people. However, some of them can be sociopaths and that may be totally something to avoid.

Don't forget that egotistical people should be avoided. They are only focused on themselves even to the detriment of others and that will drain you. Avoid having a long conversation with people like them, because all they can talk about is what they are doing and centre the whole conversation around themselves leaving you drained at the end of a conversation with them. Although If they are important to you, you can give them time to listen. This is what they need so they can be receptive to healing. However, if they defy your efforts and remain toxic or exhausting then break ties with them as soon as you can.

CHAPTER TWELVE: AVOIDING ENERGY DRAINERS

Apart from energy vampires and narcissists, there are other category of people you will need to protect yourself from. They necessarily do not fall into any defined category. This is not to damage your relationships with people because as you must have noticed, there are a lot of people around you who tend to drain you of energy. An empath unlike every other person, gets drained easily and that is why you need to be extra careful of your relationships. Most times your intuition prompts you to avoid certain persons. You need to learn to trust your guts. You can also double check with a friend that is sincere as we have said earlier. When you see people exhibit the following tendencies or tend to show any of the following characters I am about to explain, you should know it is time to protect yourself from people like them.

Empaths tend to be burden bearers and this makes you prone to needy people who do not relent in seeking for your help any day and anytime. This kind of people will do any and everything to get your attention. They are always asking for your help and consulting you for advice. Worse still, they never make use of the advice that you give them. You have to limit the time you spend with such people to avoid draining your energy. These are also the kind of people you should know when to say "no" to.

Similar to needy people are people who always get into trouble. There is always something wrong going on in their lives and they keep running to you for solutions. These people are always faced with serious problems that get you bothered every time and leaves you restless until you solve their problems. For every time you solve their problems, they are already presenting the latest dilemma of their life. This is where setting boundaries and discerning your feelings come to play. Being around this kind of people, will always cause you emotional and even physical pain leaving you with little or no energy left. You will need to figure out your energy centre and source. Engage in practices that helps you focus on your energy centre and allows you to gradually shake off negative energies by this set of people discussed.

Empaths themselves can be their own energy vampires because they are prone to be people pleasers. It can be very overwhelming when you are making attempt to please everyone. This is because it is impossible to succeed at such endeavours. You should attract people who have the same mind-set with you or people with positive energy. However, you should not try to please everyone because you will end up draining yourself of your energy.

Noises and bright light can be exhausting for empaths too. In your home, you can always furnish your room with dim light. Candles are also good for meditation. You can always stay away from noisy or crowded places too. At your workplace, you should position yourself in places where you can avoid noises to enhance productivity. If you cannot avoid noise, you can use headsets or earphones to listen to sounds with calming effects. Stay away from blasting sirens.

From all we have discussed in this chapter, empaths must take note of their relationships and the energies around them. You will need to find people who are positive, secure and confident to relate with. You should build solid and rewarding relationships with people who are mentally and emotionally balanced. You do not have to worry about attracting the right people because empaths have a unique and extremely enchanting personality. Empaths are lovely and lovable.

Never forget that you pose as a unique gift to the world so don't waste time with people who will put out your light and deprive you from shining. Avoid people who are too negative. Shut your ears and hearts from people who will drain you of your energy. You can give people a second chance and when a person keeps behaving in a way that is detrimental to you, steer clear. Know when it is alright to let people into your life. Learn how to say "no" when you should. You don't need to be angry with people. You just have to set boundaries and be firm with it.

CHAPTER THIRTEEN: DARK PSYCHOLOGY: COMMON MANIPULATION TECHNIQUES

Although it is believed that everyone must have manipulated another person at one point or the other. You must have flattered somebody to worm your way into somebody's heart for a favour or you most have told a white lie to your boss to cover up for your irresponsibility. Whether this assertion is correct or not is not the aim of this part of the book. Our world is fashioned in a way that people do not believe in dealing with people honestly or sincerely, rather they believe they have to work their ways to get what they want from people.

Interestingly, manipulation do not work for everyone. Whoever wants to employ the art of manipulation will target certain kinds of people who can easily fall for their trick. Most people who fall prey to manipulators are usually those who are not confident, who have low self-esteem or those who are naïve and inexperienced. Uniquely, another set of people who fall victim to manipulation are extremely compassionate or emotional people. Your guess is correct! Empaths can be vulnerable too.

While the manipulator may not see anything wrong in these acts, and subsequently achieves what he wants. The empath who is highly sensitive in nature gets affected above surface level and this can be very overwhelming. This may also cause an empath to lose him or herself while trying to reach for the heights in shining his or her light to the world. This is a guide to help empaths realize certain techniques people can use to manipulate them. Most of the things to do to avoid such has been discussed earlier but this is to show them various acts of manipulation people employ. Let's take a brief look at few of these techniques:

1.   **THE VICTIM ROLE:**

The manipulator will try to play the victim to get people's sympathy and compassion from people around them. It is known that people, empaths inclusive; are easily drawn to victims.

2.   **FEIGNING LOVE:**

Everyone looks for welcoming hands and warm hearts. Love is one way to easily get into the hearts of people. Manipulators especially psychopaths who do not know how to love may feign such feeling to get what they want from people.

3.   **AGGRESSION:**

Are you surprised? People often use anger and aggression to trick others into submission. This works when their preys get confused at the sudden outburst and diverts their attention to suppressing the anger other than the issue at hand.

4.   **FLATTERY:**

There is a high probability that you have once belonged to a side of the coin before or even both. You must have been flattered or you have flattered someone to get what you want. Possibly, both may have happened to you before. This is one of the most common form of manipulation where people shower praises and flattering words to get what they want. You know, words get to people easily.

5.   GUILT TRIPPING:

Not so many people know how to play the blame game. However, there are a lot of people who have gained mastery in this art. It is about pushing the blame or fault to the victim and making them look selfish or more advantaged. This ends up in confusing the victim. Other manipulators employ such techniques as downplaying their actions, lying, having frequent mood swings, love bombing, punishment, denial, twisting the truth, playing innocence, diversion and sarcasm.

CHAPTER FOURTEEN: GETTING

HEALED

The journey of an empath discovering his sense of self and ability to maximise his unique abilities comes with its own challenges as well. We have been able to view the empaths lifestyle from a balanced view. We have learnt his unique traits, his abilities and the things he needs to protect himself from. However, there are certain physical illness that is common with empaths such as chronic pain, cold, anxiety, fatigue and depression. Most empaths are experiencing these common illnesses or are prone to experiencing them. An empowered empath needs to learn how to manage these common illnesses. This part of the book covers how an empath can get healed of some of this common illnesses or pain he or she experiences.

Empaths tend to suffer from back problems and digestive disorders as well. They tend to feel the emotions of others in the centre of the abdomen which is where the solar chakra is located. The emotions they feel here weakens the centre of the abdomen and can lead to irritable

bowel syndrome, stomach ulcers and lower back problems. The empath who has not learnt how to manage the emotions they feel or who has not learnt how to reduce the impact of the emotions of others on him or her will typically suffer from such physical problems. As we said in the early chapters of this book, empaths have the tendency to pick the illness of others quickly and they tend to also develop the physical symptoms of those around them due to their nature. They often develop a range of physical illnesses or pain which include the flu, eye infections, body sores and pains in the body and bones. Empaths who are also caregivers or are taking care of anyone who has a physical illness can also develop the pains felt by that person when they are close to them.

The good news is that empaths can get healed. Let me tell you the beautiful aspect of empaths getting healed, it is the fact is that there are quite a number of natural remedies that can be used to get healing. Some people have recommended various stones and crystals which can be used for healing. There are also certain flower and Bach remedies that studies have shown as effective natural remedies which can be employed for healing by an empath or for an empath. Also, empaths are natural healers which suggests that they can direct their energies into healing themselves and others. This will help you know the steps to take whenever you experience the things that hurt you. You can also extend these recommended techniques for getting healed to other empaths or non-empaths who are facing the pain.

The process of getting healed requires the first step of you admitting that you have a particular problem. If you have not figured it out yet, go back to practicing our self-reflection techniques to figure out how exactly you may be feeling. If you are not yet feeling any of the symptoms to be addressed in this chapter, it is still good you learn for subsequent times. Are you trying to shy away from embracing your gift because you don't want to experience these things mentioned here? You may need to go back to reading about understanding your gift in the second chapter of this book. You may have started feeling some of these symptoms even naturally before knowing about your unique gift as an empath. Whichever position you stand, I will recommend that you read through this part of the book because it will come handy as a powerful tool on your discovery journey to finding one's sense of self and becoming an empowered and pain-free empath.

EMPATHS GETTING HEALED OF INSOMNIA, DEPRESSION, EXHAUSTION AND ADRENAL

FATIGUE.

Some of the major challenges faced by empaths is developing insomnia- which is a sleeping disorder that causes people's inability to have a sound or restful sleep. This can easily be caused by bearing overload of sad emotions from tragic incidences an empaths experience or hearing about a tragic situation or watching tragic or violent scenes on the television. The lack of good sleep by an empath will deprive him of the ability to let go of destructive energy. This is what makes meditation at night before sleeping important. It is shown that empaths find it difficult to sleep at night because their minds are over-burdened and they are unable to process and make sense of all the previous experience they have had in the day. There are some natural remedies which can be used to heal insomnia. These natural remedies will be discussed later.

Also, exhaustion and adrenal fatigue go hand in hand. Due to the emotional obligations that empaths are exposed to by nature, they become a dumping site for other people's sad emotions and negative energies. This usually makes them experience a sudden drop in their energy causing them to be exhausted or to experience what is known as chronic or adrenal fatigue which is a state of extreme tiredness that a person experience.

Such frequent feeling of exhaustion or tiredness coupled with an empaths lack of understanding of the source of his pain can also cause such a person to fall into depression. This further re-iterates the essence of this book. An empath need to understand his true nature and also locate his focus or his energy source for strength. While he goes through the daily challenges, he ought to know what to do on a day-to-day basis to relieve him of those challenges. In the case where he gets hurt or feel some pains or go into depression, he is to understand how he is feeling and then seek for a remedy to his problem.

The empaths hyperactive mind set is why it is possible for the empath to experience this challenge discussed above. All of these symptoms discussed above can be controlled and managed. An empath needs to always remain grounded, balanced and consciously aware of their energies and themselves. Knowing fully well that they can be a source of energy to others. Here are some of the natural remedies the empath can employ for his healing or for the healing of others.

NATURAL HEALING REMEDIES FOR EMPATHS

1. Water:

As an empath being hydrated is really important for you. Water remains one of the most essential natural resources with great healing tendencies. Studies show that water makes up about 75% of our body. It is also an excellent cleanser to get rid of toxins and to stay hydrated. We will be looking at both the benefits of drinking and bathing for empaths.

For drinking, it is recommended that you drink up to 8

-10 glasses of "pure" water a day. Take note that this is

not a recommendation for all liquids but water itself.

The water you drink has an internal cleansing effect

and the heavier you feel, the more you need water.

Taking a lot of water will allow those emotions to catch

a ride on the water to flow right out of your body. You

can also make your water work well for you by

blessing it. Thank the spirit for the water and tell it you

love it. This changes its crystalline composition on a

sub atomic level.

For bathing, taking a long luxurious bath can always

help you gain calmness. One good habit you can always

practice is having a good bath If you are feeling heavy

and drained. If you have just left a situation where you

have picked up a negative energy practice the habit of

taking a shower upon returning home. You can also add the regular sea salt or Epsom salt for your bathing. It has been studied that the Magnesium in the Epsom Salts has a very calming effect on the body. This will help you detoxify and neutralize any negative energy you may have picked up and attract negative ions from your energy field to be washed down the drain. You can also go swimming frequently because whether we are drinking a lot of water, or soaking our self in a warm bath or living by an ocean, water energizes us.

2. OILS:

Yes! Essential oils have a healing effect for empaths which is known from ancient cultures. Essential oils have a range of benefits. It can be used as antidepressants, anti- insomnia, antiseptic, and antifungals. Essential oils have a calming effect on empaths, it can reduce anxiety for those with spiritual hypersensitivity. A research was conducted by the American College of Healthcare Sciences in 2014,

They gave 58 hospice patients a daily hand massage for one week using a blend of essential oils. The oil blend was made up of lavender, frankincense and bergamot. The studies show that all the patients reported less depression and pain as a result of the essential oil massages.

The effective way of using the essential oils to achieve the healing effect include through massages. Another method is aromatherapy. This is through smelling the aroma of the oils in the bath, through the water vapor that comes from the oil, direct inhalation, a cologne or perfume made from the oil, or aromatherapy diffusers.

Another means of application is through consuming the oils orally. However, you must ensure that the oils are safe.

Some of the essential oils recommended for empaths are;

- Lavender oil reduces anxiety and stress, restores the nervous system, provides inner peace, causes better sleep, reduction in panic attacks, irritability and general nervous tension.

- Rose Oil also takes away depression, anxiety, grieving, shock and panic attacks.

- Vetiver oil contains good energy for grounding and self-awareness. It is also used for reducing panic attacks, shocks, trauma or anxiety.

- Bergamot oil provides soothing energy that induces relaxation, reduces anxiety, and heals insomnia, and can be an anti-depressant.

- Ylang Ylang also reduces depression, to reduce anxiety, to induce optimism, enhance cheerfulness, and courage. It can also serve as a sedative to heal insomnia.

- Frankincense oil is a great use for meditation. It can also be used for treating anxiety, depression and to achieve calming effects.

3. FLOWERS AND HERBS:

Flower Remedies includes the application of products gotten from plants, trees or flowers to reduce one's exposure to pain, anxiety and fatigue which are the most common symptoms empaths encounter in their day to day living. There are also herbs that are beneficial to empaths and they can help to stimulate, adapt to stress, rest and relax the nerves. Examples of these include; the Vervain, the Gotu Kola, the Maca Root, Matcha green tea and Raw Cacao for those who love caffeine. By either inhaling or drinking these herbal tea, the empath experiences a drastic reduction of tension and anxiety. In addition to these is substituting your intake of caffeine and other seeming energy boosters to taking in materials that have a high vitamin and minerals concentration.

Having learnt earlier about the chakras and their essence to an empaths' connection to his real nature, these aspects of flower and herbs remedies would be incomplete without talking about herbs that can help purify and neutralize the chakras.

These herbs include the Ashwangadha- which helps an empath develop a sense of security and safety, there is also Damiana which helps to enhance creativity and to heal empaths of most of the common physical illnesses experienced by empaths. There is a long list of others herbs which nature has bestowed for the healing process of an empath.

The flower remedies also come in handy for all empaths. Uniquely the flower remedies which are sometimes known as the flower essence entails various flower products each having its own distinct healing property embedded in itself. I will highly recommend a further study to these remedies and see how each works to address whatever feeling or pain that you encounter. There has also been product of extensive scientific studies that came up with a natural solution made from dewdrops of these flowers which are known as the Bach Flower Remedies. They include; the Cerato, chicory, Gorse among others.

4. CRYSTALS:

Crystals are a three dimensioned patterned object composed of an array of atoms possessing long range order. They are also known as gemstones. It is believed that crystals are useful for empaths because they are a direct link to Mother Nature and they help to create balance during meditations. Crystals are used to protect against hypersensitivity, stress, anxiety, emotional distress, and danger. It helps them remember the earth frequencies and starts to vibrate with the crystalline energy. It is known that the specific crystals for empaths are PREHNITE, which allows empaths to cleanse the negative energy not belonging to them and allows you to detach the links you have with such negative aura. BLACK TOURMALINE has a protective shield that protects the energy. HALITE is also a powerful mineral for empaths which helps to enhance their psychic abilities and removes negativity.

You can place these crystals in your home, or on your desk at your workplace and can be useful holding it during meditations or grounding to counter negative energy around you.

In place of real crystals, you can pick a calming scene or color for design on your walls, or as your desktop wallpaper. You can also use a photo frame or uplifting picture and keep it on your

desk. Focusing on these designs or pictures at

intervals will help you maintain focus and

generate positive energy.

CONCLUSION

As much as this book has completely covered all you need to know about being an empath. There are certainly more things for you to discover. Everyone keeps learning, including empaths. Your journey to full knowledge has just started. Be prepared to meet challenges and circumstances this book didn't mention. Even though this is a possibility, I believe this book has however prepared you for even such times.

Now you know that it is alright to feel the way you feel and you make a beautiful part of the puzzle of existence. Like every other person, you matter and you are valuable. You can manage your emotions and your sensitivities. You have learnt to embrace your gift fully and let people know how much of a gift you are to them. You now know it is okay not to feel alright and up to it all the time but you now know how to get re-energized and that is more important.

The empaths nature relates to everything including their jobs, habits and relationships. You now know what is good and what is not. You are gradually learning how to say no and not feeling bad about it. You can now navigate through life not just as a mirror reflecting other people's energy but as one who knows how to walk and not get hurt. Even when you get hurt, you are able to tap into nature's gift for healing. You are able to achieve all that you want from life and can always be happy.

I believe empaths are true gifts to mankind. I hope you now believe the same as well. The empaths' lifestyle is truly a blessing and not a curse as some people may attribute it. It is a life worthy of being explored because of its unique gifts to the world. One thing that makes it fulfilling is fully understanding the nature of the gift and making a lifelong decision to develop one's unique abilities and to take every required step of finding one's sense of self.

I know reading this book has been an eventful journey to living, to purpose, to healing, to success and happiness. I am glad you came along. I hope you take note of all the details and heed to all action steps you need to take to get the most out of this nature.